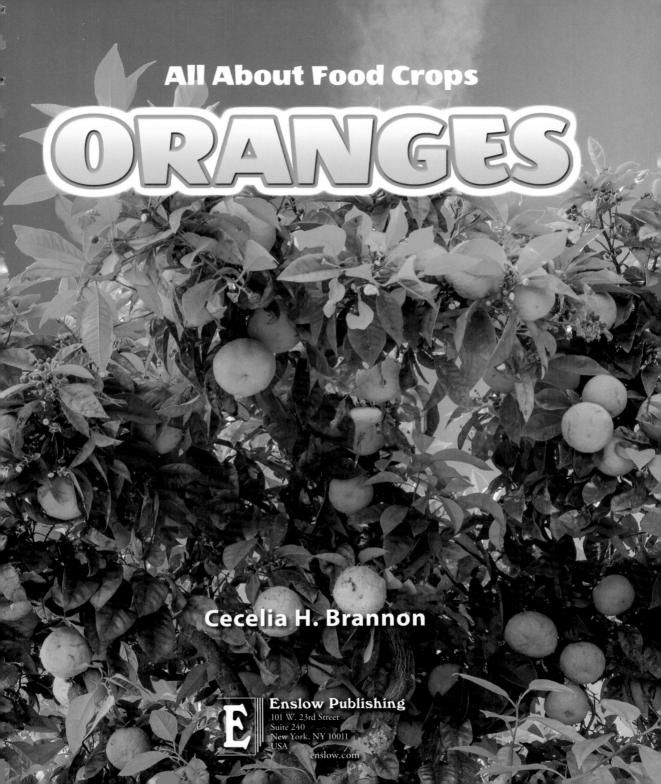

All About Food Crops

ORANGES

Cecelia H. Brannon

Enslow Publishing
101 W. 23rd Street
Suite 240
New York, NY 10011
USA
enslow.com

Published in 2018 by Enslow Publishing, LLC
101 W. 23rd Street, Suite 240, New York, NY 10011

Library of Congress Cataloging-in-Publication Data

Names: Brannon, Cecelia H., author. | Brannon, Cecelia H. All about food crops.
Title: Oranges / Cecelia H. Brannon.
Description: New York, NY : Enslow Publishing, 2018. | Series: All about food crops | Audience: Pre-K to grade 1. | Includes bibliographical references and index.
Identifiers: LCCN 2017002023| ISBN 9780766085817 (library-bound) | ISBN 9780766088276 (pbk.) | ISBN 9780766088214 (6-pack)
Subjects: LCSH: Oranges—Juvenile literature.
Classification: LCC SB370.O7 B73 2018 | DDC 634/.31—dc23
LC record available at https://lccn.loc.gov/2017002023

Printed in the United States of America

To Our Readers: We have done our best to make sure all websites in this book were active and appropriate when we went to press. However, the author and the publisher have no control over and assume no liability for the material available on those websites or on any websites they may link to. Any comments or suggestions can be sent by email to customerservice@enslow.com.

Photo Credits: Cover, p. 1 Ewais/Shutterstock.com; pp. 3 (left), 8 photosbyjim/iStock/Thinkstock; pp. 3 (center), 20 Maria Uspenskaya/Shutterstock.com; pp. 3 (right), 6 Deborah Lee Rossiter/ Shutterstock.com; pp. 4–5 Rickythai/Shutterstock.com; p. 10 Stock Montage/Archive Photos/ Getty Images; p. 12 Lori Skelton/Shutterstock.com; p. 14 Tatiana Volgutova/Shutterstock.com; p. 16 Iryna Denysova/Shutterstock.com; p. 18 Diana Taliun/Shutterstock.com; p. 22 Gladskikh Tatiana/ Shutterstock.com.

Contents

Words to Know

blossom   citrus   evergreen

Oranges are an important crop.

4

Orange trees are evergreens. This means the leaves are always green!

When many orange trees are grown together, it is called a grove. Their flowers are called orange blossoms.

Christopher Columbus was a famous explorer. He first brought oranges to America from Spain in 1493.

Most of the oranges in the world are grown in Brazil. But Florida grows the most oranges in the United States.

Oranges, their blossoms, and their peels are used to make teas, jams, and juice!

The nice-smelling fruit and blossoms are also used to make perfumes, creams, and soaps.

There are more than 600 kinds of orange. One kind is the blood orange, which is red!

Oranges are the most popular citrus fruit in the world. Citrus fruit are sour or tangy, like lemons, limes, and grapefruits.

Oranges taste good! They are good for you, too!

Read More

Rattini, Kristin Baird. *National Geographic Readers: Seed to Plant.* Washington, DC: National Geographic, 2014.

Staniford, Linda. *Where Does Fruit Come From?* Portsmouth, NH: Heinemann, 2016.

Websites

Kids Cooking Activities
www.kids-cooking-activities.com/orange-facts.html
Check out some tasty orange recipes to try with an adult.

Science Kids
www.sciencekids.co.nz/sciencefacts/food/oranges.html
Learn more facts about oranges.

Index

Guided Reading Level: C
Guided Reading Leveling System is based on the guidelines recommended by Fountas and Pinnell.

Word Count: 146